What If?

What If the Hole in the Ozone Layer Grows Larger?

Holly Cefrey

HIGH
interest
books

Children's Press®
A Division of Scholastic Inc.
New York / Toronto / London / Auckland / Sydney
Mexico City / New Delhi / Hong Kong
Danbury, Connecticut

Book Design: Michael DeLisio and Michelle Innes
Contributing Editor: Matthew Pitt

Photo Credits: Cover © Dave G. Houser/Corbis (illustrative enhancement by Michael DeLisio); pp. 4, 7, 8, 17, 21, 23, 33, 34 © SpaceScapes/Photodisc; pp. 5, 6, 10, illustrations by Michael DeLisio; p. 6 © Michael Pole/Corbis; p. 6 © Michael Pole/Corbis; p. 9 (Mountain image used in diagram) © Visions of Nature/Corbis Royalty Free; p. 13 illustration by Michael DeLisio with © SpaceScapes/Photodisc; p. 14 top and bottom © NASA; p. 16 © Galen Rowell/Corbis; p. 18 © Jim Sugar Photography/Corbis; p. 20 © Craig Lovell/Corbis; p. 22 © Sandie Gibbs/Corbis; pp. 24, 26, 32 © Ted Spiegel/Corbis; p. 29 © Reflections Photolibrary/Corbis; p. 31 © Eye Ubiquitous/Corbis; p. 35 © David and Peter Turnley/Corbis; p. 36 © Sally Morgan/Corbis; p. 39 © Gail Mooney/Corbis; p. 40 © Richard T. Nowitz/Corbis

Library of Congress Cataloging-in-Publication Data

Cefrey, Holly.
What if the hole in the ozone layer grows larger? / Holly Cefrey.
    p. cm. -- (What if?)
Includes bibliographical references and index.
Summary: Introduces environmental issues relating to the causes and effects of the
    hole in the ozone layer.
ISBN 0-516-23913-9 (lib. bdg.) -- ISBN 0-516-23476-5 (pbk.)
1. Ozone layer depletion--Juvenile literature. 2. Ozone layer depletion--
    Environmental aspects--Juvenile literature. [1. Ozone layer depletion.] I. Title.
    II. What if? (Children's Press)

QC879.712 .C44 2002
363.738'75--dc21

                                                                        2001042352

CONTENTS

INTRODUCTION

January 1, 2230—A message from the president of the United States:

"*Good evening, my fellow Americans. I deliver this message tonight with a hopeful heart. I have learned some wonderful news from our top scientists.*

"*As you know, the people of Earth have not always lived underground. At one time, lush green plants covered our planet's surface. People walked freely under beautiful blue skies. No one feared the Sun. All that changed when the ozone layer disappeared. We learned, too late, how important the ozone layer was. We learned that the layer protected us and made our world livable. The powerful Sun shone down, but did not cause the diseases and destruction that it does today.*

"*Now, we can't go above ground without wearing special suits and goggles. No plants can grow, and the temperatures change wildly, without warning.*

The surface air is unbreathable.

"I am pleased to say that we are finally recovering from the mistakes of the past. Our best scientists now believe we will soon be able to leave our underground homes and return to Earth's surface. Someday, our children could feel the warmth of real sunlight on their skin—a feeling you and I have never known. Let us hope that this dream will come true."

This fictional speech could be from a scene in our future. The threat of losing the ozone layer is real. Some of the Sun's rays are very harmful to living things. The ozone layer blocks these harmful rays known as UV, or ultraviolet, rays. Without the ozone layer, UV rays would reach Earth's surface, damaging all forms of life.

What do we really know about ozone? What will happen if the ozone layer disappears? What steps can we take to save it? In this book, we will learn the answers to these questions.

CHAPTER ONE

Hole in the Sky

WHAT'S THE MATTER?

All things in the universe are made up of one or more forms of matter. There are three main forms of matter: gases, solids, and liquids. Gases, such as ozone and oxygen, are free-moving substances. Solids, such as rocks, are structured substances. Liquids, such as water, are fluid substances. Water can turn into a gas called water vapor.

Water vapor, ozone, and oxygen are some of the many gases that make up our air. This combination of gases also makes up the air in the atmosphere above us.

A healthy balance of gases in our atmosphere helps warm Earth. Without it, our planet would be left frozen and lifeless.

Special Coating

The atmosphere is made up of several layers of gases, which coat the entire Earth. Our atmosphere protects us. It gives us air to breathe and provides fresh water. The atmosphere also balances Earth's temperature. It uses sunlight to make heat, which warms the surface of Earth. This is called the "greenhouse effect."

SKY STUFF

There are many different layers of the atmosphere. Some of these layers include:

Troposphere—0-7 miles (0-12 km) above Earth
  • Contains mostly water vapor and other gases

Stratosphere—7-30 miles (12-50 km) above Earth
  • Contains the ozone layer

Mesosphere—30-50 miles (50-80 km) above Earth

Thermosphere—50-372 miles (80-600 km) above Earth

Exosphere—372-430 miles (600-692 km) above Earth
  • The upper layer of our atmosphere

Earth's protective shield of gases extends far above the surface, as this image shows.

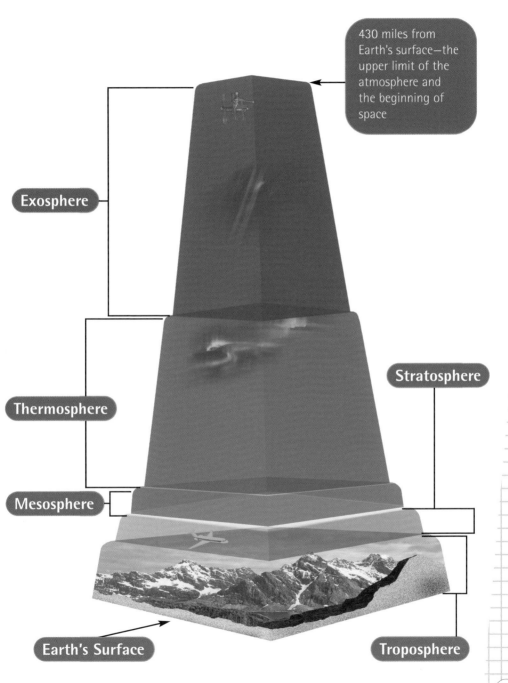

430 miles from Earth's surface—the upper limit of the atmosphere and the beginning of space

Exosphere

Stratosphere

Thermosphere

Mesosphere

Troposphere

Earth's Surface

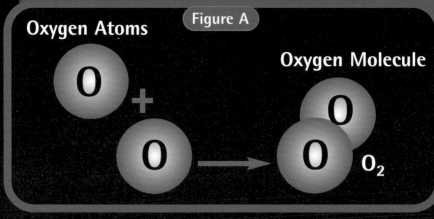

Oxygen Atoms Figure A

O + O → O O O₂ **Oxygen Molecule**

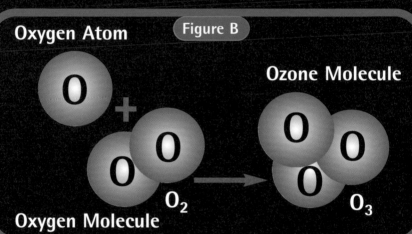

Oxygen Atom Figure B

O + O O O₂ → O O O O₃ **Ozone Molecule**

Oxygen Molecule

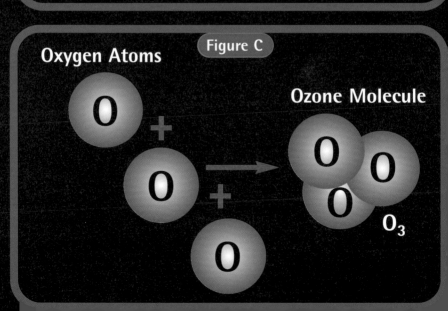

Oxygen Atoms Figure C

O + O + O → O O O O₃ **Ozone Molecule**

Without the atmosphere, sunlight would simply bounce off Earth and return to space. Then Earth's surface would be below freezing. Nothing would be able to survive.

THE UV EFFECT

Everything is made of atoms. Atoms are the smallest independent parts of matter. When two or more atoms join together, they create a molecule. Molecules can split apart into single atoms. These atoms can then rejoin to make the same molecule again. Or, they can join other atoms to make other kinds of molecules.

Ozone gas is made from the same oxygen atoms that make up the air we breathe. When two oxygen atoms combine, they form an oxygen molecule that becomes part of the air we breathe (Figure A). When three oxygen atoms combine, an ozone molecule is formed (Figures B and C).

UV rays can split the two atoms of an oxygen molecule apart. When this happens, the two oxygen atoms move freely. A free oxygen atom can join with another

This diagram demonstrates the process of oxygen and ozone formation.

single oxygen atom. When this happens, oxygen is made again. If a free oxygen atom joins an oxygen molecule—which already has two oxygen atoms—an ozone molecule is formed.

Ozone molecules can be split apart by UV rays, too. Both ozone and oxygen molecules are found in the ozone layer. The process of splitting oxygen and ozone molecules apart

Did You Know?

Scientists made their first official measurements of the Antarctic ozone loss in 1985. But the results were so shocking that the scientists weren't sure whether their instruments were giving them the correct information!

exhausts all of the energy contained in UV rays. This prevents many harmful UV rays from reaching the Earth.

The ozone layer is like a big safety net far above Earth. It catches UV rays before they can reach Earth and hurt humans and other animals. As long as we have both ozone and oxygen in our atmosphere, the UV rays are stopped at the ozone layer.

Acting as a protective "net," the ozone layer prevents UV rays from reaching Earth's surface, or at least it should. Where the net is thin or has disappeared, UV rays break through.

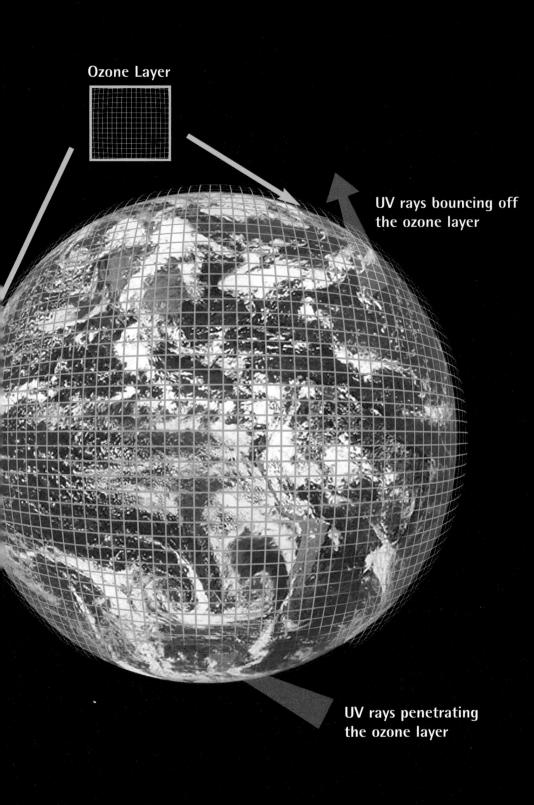

Ozone Layer

UV rays bouncing off
the ozone layer

UV rays penetrating
the ozone layer

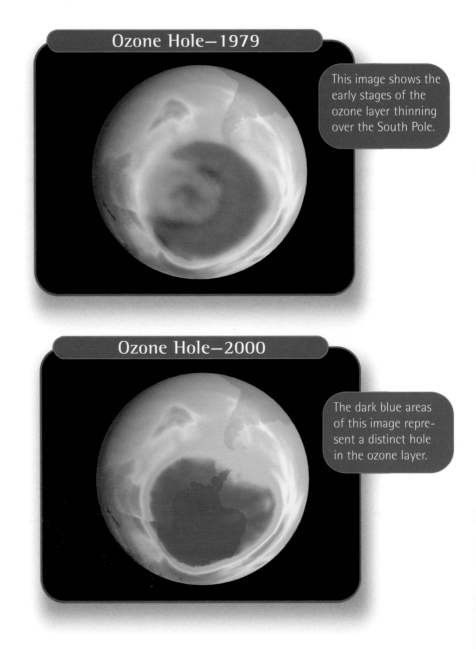

Ozone Hole—1979

This image shows the early stages of the ozone layer thinning over the South Pole.

Ozone Hole—2000

The dark blue areas of this image represent a distinct hole in the ozone layer.

A SCARY DISCOVERY

In the late 1970s, the British Antarctic Survey (BAS) made a scary discovery. The part of the ozone layer over the South Pole and Antarctica was very thin. It was missing ozone gas. In pictures of Earth taken by satellites in space, this area looks like a hole.

Since this discovery, scientists have kept a close watch on the hole. It isn't always there. It comes and goes with the changing seasons. During September and October, the hole appears. More than 50 percent of the ozone gas is missing during this time. A few months later, the hole disappears. Yet each year it returns, often larger than before.

According to the National Aeronautic and Space Administration (NASA), the hole reached its largest size ever in September 2000. The hole was three times larger than the United States!

No hole exists over the Arctic or the North Pole. However, that area has a problem too. The ozone layer over the Arctic thins slightly in January and February. If we're not careful, this could be the start of another hole.

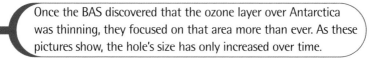

Once the BAS discovered that the ozone layer over Antarctica was thinning, they focused on that area more than ever. As these pictures show, the hole's size has only increased over time.

CHAPTER TWO

Enemies of Ozone

After the hole was discovered, scientists rushed to find the cause. They found that the damage done to the ozone layer was due to a loss of oxygen. Scientists believe humans are responsible for much of this oxygen loss. As the atmosphere continues to lose oxygen, the amount of ozone suffers, too.

Here's how it works. Plants and trees make oxygen and release it into the air. When plant life is destroyed, fewer oxygen atoms are released. Remember that oxygen atoms are needed to make ozone molecules. If fewer oxygen atoms are in the air, less ozone can be made. The longer this happens, the larger the holes in our ozone safety net become! Without our ozone safety net, it's easier for dangerous UV rays to reach us.

Using tools like this ozone balloon, scientists can measure how much precious ozone our atmosphere has lost.

ATTACKING OZONE

Pollution is another reason for oxygen loss. Automobiles, air conditioners, factories, and power stations cause pollution. Pollution adds harmful gases and particles—such as dust, soot, and ash—to the air. Polluted air damages both oxygen and ozone. Two kinds of gas molecules in polluted air cause the most ozone loss. These are CFCs and halon gas molecules.

CFC is the short form of the word *chlorofluorocarbon*. CFCs are used in things such as aerosols, air conditioners, cleaning products, and refrigerators. CFCs were created fifty years ago. They don't harm humans directly. In fact, we first used CFCs to replace other, more toxic gases. But over time, CFCs have had a dangerous effect: They damage the atmosphere's ozone layer.

When CFCs are released into the air, they slowly travel toward the stratosphere. Experts at the Environmental Protection Agency (EPA) say that it may take many years for one CFC molecule to make this long journey. Yet when it reaches its destination, it is very destructive. While in the stratosphere, a CFC

Today's snarls of traffic can make for minor headaches. But the pollutants produced by cars and trucks will make Mother Earth sick for many more tomorrows.

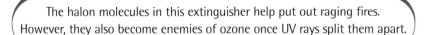

The halon molecules in this extinguisher help put out raging fires. However, they also become enemies of ozone once UV rays split them apart.

molecule is exposed to UV rays. These UV rays break apart the molecule. One of its atoms, called the chlorine atom, is released. It moves about freely. It breaks apart any ozone molecules that it finds. During its time in the ozone layer, one single chlorine atom can destroy more than 100,000 ozone molecules!

Halon molecules, which are found in the chemicals used in fire extinguishers, also travel to the stratosphere. They are even more destructive than CFCs. When UV rays split apart a halon molecule, a bromine atom is released. The bromine atom is ten times more powerful than the chlorine atom. Halon and CFC molecules destroy ozone faster than nature can replace it.

SKY STUFF

Getting Warmer

Global warming is the unnatural rise of air temperature near Earth's surface. The same CFC gases that harm the ozone layer are partially to blame for global warming.

Our atmosphere already traps heat for us naturally. Polluting gases trap more heat. As people release more and more polluting gases into the air, too much heat is trapped. This causes temperatures to rise. Many scientists fear that as polluting gases build up, Earth and the atmosphere will become warmer and warmer. This will most likely melt the polar ice caps, causing massive flooding around the globe.

CHAPTER THREE

Cycle of Destruction

FUTURE OF OZONE LOSS

Scientists keep careful watch on ozone levels and the ozone hole. In doing so, they learn more about the problem. They've discovered that the amount of ozone gas is always less at the North and South Poles than in other places. Harmful gases destroy ozone much faster in extremely cold temperatures. This is why the hole formed above Antarctica, instead of over North America, Europe, or other warm areas around the world.

However, the poles aren't the only places that lose ozone. According to the EPA, satellites show that the ozone layer is becoming thinner over the entire globe.

If this happens, what will it mean for humans?

NASA's scientists use this probe, known as HALOE, to locate areas where the ozone layer has thinned or vanished.

Right now, we have a large supply of fresh water, plants, food, and air. Earth, the Sun, and the atmosphere provide these things through a continual cycle. This cycle is dependable, but it's also delicate. When one part of the cycle suffers, the rest does too. Think about what happens when toxic chemicals are spilled in a pond. Plant and animal life is greatly disturbed. The same thing will happen on a larger scale if Earth's air quality gets more polluted. As the air gets dirtier, plants will die, and other things will follow. There will be less oxygen released into the air for us to breathe. And finally, there will be less ozone protection.

CHANGING LIFE ON EARTH

We know that without the ozone layer, huge amounts of UV rays would reach Earth. What could the effects of this ozone loss be? Based on what we know about UV rays, we can guess what might happen.

- UV rays would prevent us from getting enough food. UV rays damage crops that we depend on for food. UV rays also cause tiny organisms and plants in the oceans to die. This would set off a chain reaction.

Without the ozone layer to protect Earth's crops, UV rays will damage or even destroy them.

Larger sea animals depend on these organisms and plants for food. As the marine world starved to death, land animals that eat fish to survive would suffer, too. As food became scarce, people might panic. Riots might occur, which could affect the governments of countries.

- UV rays would affect our breathing. More UV rays reaching Earth's surface would lead to more ozone at the surface. While ozone is a necessary ally for the atmosphere, it can harm humans when produced near Earth's surface. Many areas would be blanketed by smog. Smog could increase to deadly levels. Also, because plant life was harmed, the amount of breathable oxygen would shrink.

- UV rays would harm our bodies. UV rays already cause sunburns and skin cancer. UV rays also weaken immune systems and cause damage to our eyes. Massive amounts of UV rays would lead to many more illnesses and deaths. In parts of Chile and Argentina, damage to the ozone layer is forcing people indoors. Leaders of these nations have told people to avoid going outside during midday. This is

Thanks to UV rays and smog, some of our most glorious city skylines are fading from view.

when the sun is at its strongest. When people do go outside, they must wear hats, sunscreen, and protective clothing to fight the UV rays. And experts at NASA are worried that holes in the ozone safety net are appearing everywhere. Recent discoveries suggest that the ozone hole may soon spread to parts of the United States and Canada.

Here are details on some health hazards that UV rays might cause, if there's no ozone layer to keep them away from Earth's surface.

Skin Cancer

Scientists are certain that UV rays can cause skin cancers. People can get skin cancer if they're exposed to harmful amounts of UV rays for long periods of time.

Cells are the basic building blocks of life. UV rays damage skin cells. The cells don't die, but they are changed in a way that causes them to become unhealthy. This leads to skin cancer. As cancer develops, it can spread to other parts of the body. More than 800,000 cases of skin cancer occur in the United States each year. Over 1,000 of these result in death.

> To fight the harmful effects of UV rays, it's always a good idea to apply lots of sunscreen lotion.

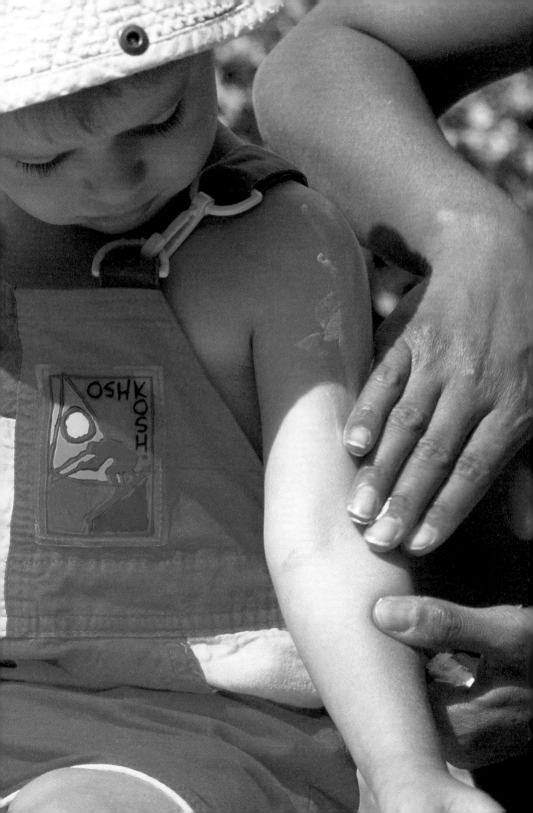

Weakened Immune System

The immune system is the body's natural shield against disease and infection. This system attacks harmful invaders such as bacteria and viruses.

UV rays can weaken the immune system, changing its ability to work properly. If the immune system is weakened, the body isn't able to fight off attack. Serious health problems, and even death, can result.

Eye Problems

Looking directly at the sun for even a few seconds can cause permanent eye damage. UV rays may not be visible, but they're very powerful. UV rays can reach our eyes by bouncing off water, sand, concrete, and snow. UV rays cause eye problems such as cataracts. A cataract is a slow clouding of the lens of the eye. The lens focuses what we see. As the lens clouds up, we begin to lose our vision.

So what can we do to keep these dangers from harming us? A lot!

Though UV rays are invisible, their effects are plain to see. Here is a young boy with cataracts in his right eye.

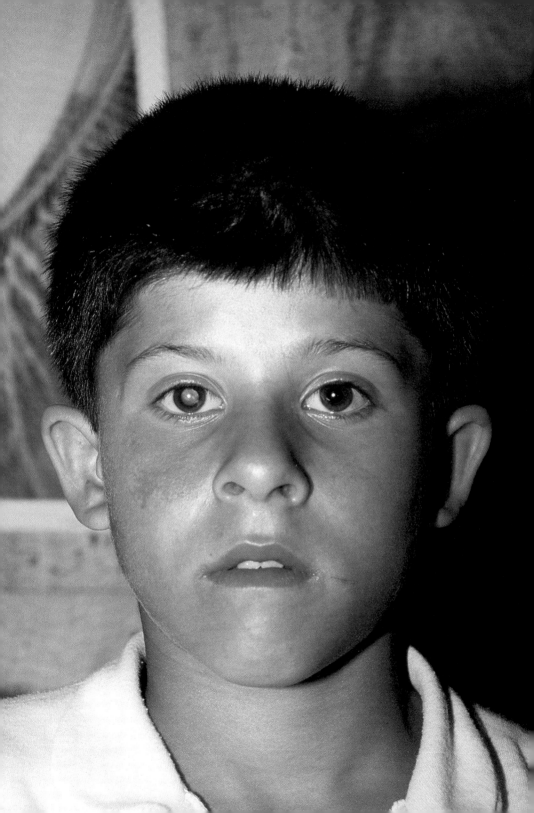

CHAPTER FOUR

Act Now!

Humans strive for a better future. Whether it's going to school, going to work, or raising a family, we think about tomorrow. This is the same approach we must use toward protecting our planet. If we ignore the needs of Earth now, we won't have a safe, clean planet in the future. What we do right now makes a big difference.

PROBLEM SOLVERS

What's happening to the ozone layer is a global problem. Nearly all of Earth's nations are responsible for polluting the air with dangerous gases. In the last twenty years, more and more people have become involved. To solve the problem and save the ozone layer, they are urging their nations' leaders to take action.

Since the ozone layer started to thin, young adults have responded to the challenge of cutting back on CFCs.

SKY STUFF

The first major global agreement between nations started in 1987. It was called the Montreal Protocol. The goal of this agreement is to phase out all CFC and halon use. Since 1987, more than 160 countries have signed the Protocol. Other measures include the following:

- 1978—The United States becomes first nation to ban all unnecessary use of CFCs in aerosols
- 1985—Vienna Convention for Protection of the Ozone Layer: For the first time, nations agreed to study an environmental problem before its effects were proven
- 1990—Improvements made to the EPA's Clean Air Act
- 1992—Copenhagen Agreement: Governments promised to phase out destructive CFCs by 1996

Family Matters

If these agreements are followed, the ozone hole may be fully repaired within the next sixty years. As of October 2000, the amount of CFCs in the lower

The United States' ban on CFCs in aerosols was a step in the right direction.

atmosphere has finally decreased. Even with this good news, the hole is the largest it has ever been. That's because chlorine and bromine atoms stay in the atmosphere for years before fading away. Even if we stopped using all CFCs today, their gases would still do damage for years to come. The important thing is to stop doing further damage. That's where you come in!

NASA and the EPA believe that each of us can do things to prevent further ozone loss. You and your family can work together to battle the damage being done to the ozone layer. Your efforts will also improve the quality of the air around us.

Stop CFC Leaks

Some important objects we use every day operate with CFCs. These objects can release CFCs if their seals are broken. CFC leaks can be prevented by regularly checking the seals. If your family uses the following objects, you may have CFC leaks in:
• Air conditioners
• Air-conditioned cars made before 1995
• Freezers/refrigerators

Gone but not forgotten: If the seals on these appliances have been broken, CFCs could be poisoning the sky.

You and your family can help Earth by doing the following things:
- For the home—Use ceiling fans, drapes, and window
  shades instead of air-conditioning. Also, plant trees
  near your house or apartment.
- For cars—Instead of air-conditioning, use window
  glazing. When the car is parked, cover the windshield
  with a window shade. You can also replace old CFC
  units with the newer air-conditioning systems.
- For freezers/refrigerators—If these objects need to
  be fixed, your parents can ask the repairperson to
  use recycling and recovery equipment.

To Reduce Ozone Damage
- Get rid of all the items in your house that release
  CFCs or halon gas.
- Buy fire extinguishers that use water or dry chemi-
  cals, instead of halon.
- Use roll-on or spray bottles instead of aerosol cans.
- Don't buy mattresses, insulation, furniture cush-
  ions, or carpet pads made out of foam—there are
  non-foam choices for each.

Taking mass transit instead of driving a car
is one way we can help keep Earth healthy.

- Carpool, or take the bus or train.
- Always try to reuse or recycle items.
- Avoid spilling gasoline while filling cars or lawnmowers.
- Keep the tires of the family car filled.

Sun Protection
- Cover up! Wear hats, long-sleeved shirts, and UV-blocking sunglasses.

TRASH

NO BOTTLES OR CANS

RECYCLE

GLASS ONLY

- Use sunscreen of SPF 15 or higher.
- Reapply the sunscreen every 2 hours that you're in the sun.
- Avoid the sun during its strongest hours—11 A.M. to 3 P.M.
- Be careful on cloudy days, too—the UV rays can still reach you.

When companies started using CFCs and halon gases in their products, it was a wrong and costly turn. But we're moving in the right direction now by limiting the use of these gases. Though major improvements in the ozone layer won't be seen for years, it's important that we keep working. We can make the quality of life better — not just for us, but also for those who come after us.

It will take patience and persistence to patch up the hole in the ozone layer. It is a slow process, but not a hopeless one. Without a doubt, the small things we do now can help the cycle of life continue for many more centuries.

If you don't recycle your garbage, you're only trashing the Earth.

41

atmosphere the layers of gases surrounding Earth's surface

atom the smallest part of matter

bromine atom part of the halon molecule that destroys ozone molecules

chlorine atom part of the CFC molecule that destroys ozone molecules

chlorofluorocarbon (CFC) a gas used in refrigerators, air conditioners, and aerosol sprays that destroys ozone molecules

greenhouse effect the trapping of the Sun's heat in Earth's atmosphere

halon a gas that destroys ozone molecules

immune system the body's natural shield that fights infection and disease

molecule the smallest part of a substance that is made up of one or more atoms

oxygen a gas that makes up part of the atmosphere

ozone a gas made up of three oxygen atoms

ozone hole the area of ozone loss over Antarctica

ozone layer the part of the atmosphere that blocks UV rays

ultraviolet (UV) rays invisible rays of sunlight that can, in high amounts, be damaging

FOR FURTHER READING

Edmonds, Alex. *The Ozone Hole*. Brookfield, CT: Millbrook Press, 1997.

Fisher, Marshall. *The Ozone Layer*. New York: Chelsea House Publishers, 1992.

Hoff, Mary King and Mary M. Rodgers. *Our Endangered Planet: Atmosphere*. Minneapolis, MN: The Lerner Publishing Group, 1995.

Morgan, Sally. *The Ozone Hole*. Danbury, CT: Franklin Watts, Incorporated, 1999.

Organizations

Environmental Protection Agency (EPA)
Ariel Rios Building
1200 Pennsylvania Avenue, NW
Washington, DC 20460
(202) 260-7400
Hotline: (800) 296-1996
www.epa.gov/ozone

Union of Concerned Scientists (UCS)
2 Brattle Square
Cambridge, MA 02238
(617) 547-5552
www.ucsusa.org

Web Sites

Greenpeace

www.greenpeace.org/~ozone

The site provides helpful links and describes new, Earth-friendly products, like CFC-free refrigerators.

NASA: For Kids Only

http://kids.mtpe.hq.nasa.gov

Find out how NASA studies air, land, water, and natural hazards on this site. There are also fun facts and games.

On the Trail of the Missing Ozone

www.epa.gov/kids/missing.htm

A lively and informative virtual comic book, describing the effects we can have on our environment.

The Ozone Hole Tour

www.atm.ch.cam.ac.uk/tour

There's even a link on this site to "Ask a Scientist" your questions about the ozone layer.

INDEX

INDEX

About the Author

Holly Cefrey is a freelance writer and researcher. She is a member of the Authors Guild and the Society of Children's Book Writers and Illustrators.